Proven Strategies to Increase Value and Attract Qualified Buyers

Selling Your Business

A Business Owner's Guide to the retirement you desire

David R. Shortill
2015

Thank you:

A special thank you to the Publish and Profit Community.
You know who you are.
Without your help and guidance, a guy with A.D.D. would surely spin out of control and give up on such a project.
You saw me do it.
Tons of love and respect for my life partner, Heather. Sorry for keeping you up at night and thanks for your motivation and assistance along the way.
To all of my dear and faithful customers. It has been my pleasure working with you throughout our working lives. Watching your families grow and prosper has been my ultimate reward.
To the colleagues and business partners both honest and those that stole from me, the lessons and knowledge I gained from you could fill three books.
I would especially like to thank those of you that are reading the first in my "Value of Advice" series of financial awareness books.
It is you who will be able to take advantage of other people's mistakes.
You will learn to look ahead and be prepared for what the future brings, and to take advantage of time and create a legacy of love for your family.
We are only on this planet a short while and like my new friend Azam Khan said to me...."It is not about the money, it is about doing something special with my life".
Azam is an incredibly hard working professional in the Event Catering industry and a single father of nine year old Eshan.
If there is something that you will take away from this reading, let it be to create your "legacy of love".
Also, when seeking advice be sure that it comes from someone who truly cares about your family and your well being.

Table of Contents

- Knowledge and Preparedness are Key
- Timing is Everything

Chapter 1.
Selling Your Business - Darren's Story

Chapter 2.
Ian's Story - Tips on Taxation

Chapter 3.
Ten Steps to Increase the Value of your Company

Chapter 4.
Clem's Story and the Importance of Employees

Chapter 5.
Your Company Policy with Regards to Employees

Chapter 6.
Strategic Planning and S.W.O.T.
Azam's Story

Chapter 8.
Hiring of Generation Y or "How Millennials think"

Chapter 9.
Your Business Viewpoint - A ten minute check up that will help you understand the type of work that I do as an Advisor. Your responses will help us determine how to proceed.

Knowledge and Preparedness are Key

It was a frosty February morning.
The sun was just about to rise on the flat prairie horizon.
Our death defying flight about to have its first delay.
My mission: fly my mother to Edmonton, Alberta in a Cessna 152, part of building flying time and experience towards a commercial pilot's license. I was seventeen years old.
The journey begins at St. Andrews Airport, just north of the city of Winnipeg, Manitoba.
The temperature is -30°.
If we are going to get this plane started, we will have to warm the engine with a heating blanket called a Herman Nelson.
The Herman Nelson blows warm air onto the frozen engine so as to thaw out the oil and to enable it to start.
My mom is sitting toasty warm in the car, no doubt wondering how long this will take and how it will affect our flight.
I get the Herman Nelson in place and do a visual walk around of the little two seat Cessna. Tires look good, fuel is full in both tanks, ailerons, elevator and rudder are free.
Pitot tube is clear, however there is a buildup of frost on the wings.
This means that we will have to let the rising sun burn the frost from the wings before we are going anywhere. The plan to be airborne at sun rise has taken a twist. Mom and I head to the coffee shop and wait.
The weather for the first leg of our trip is typical for February on the Prairies, sunny and cold.
Two and a half hours later we head back to the aircraft and I complete my walk around, checking to be sure the plane is airworthy.
We haul our bags and egg salad sandwiches that my father made for us the night before into the plane, taxi to position and open our flight plan.
We take off on runway 18 and pick up a heading of 270°.

First stop will be to fuel up and use the washroom in Brandon, Manitoba.

From Brandon we will fly to Regina, Saskatchewan and spend the night. Mom and I enjoyed a great dinner and even took in a movie before tucking in to the Regina Inn for a good night sleep.

We were completely oblivious to the adventures that awaited the next leg or our journey.

The next day begins with breakfast and a cab ride to the airport. The weather has warmed up to -20° and looks to be pretty good on through to Edmonton.

It was a short walk from the cab to where we had parked the aircraft beside a row of hangars the day before.

I phoned in my completed flight plan with Regina International Airport and was excited to take off.

We crawled back into the plane about 9am after a quick walk around and check of the ATIS or Automatic Terminal Information Service to get winds, active runway and altimeter setting prior to contacting ground control and taxing to the active runway. I did the pre-start check list and primed the engine, only to realize, the engine would not start.

Battery was fine, but the starter had gone.

I would now have to hand crank the propeller.

We will get this baby started and I can worry about getting it fixed in Edmonton.

I explained to my mom that I had the brakes set and that I was going to turn the propeller by hand in order to get the engine started.

I can only imagine how my mom must have felt sitting in the plane, all alone while I was outside turning the propeller.

Much like bum starting a motorcycle, if you turn the crankcase of the Lycoming engine, with the ignition on, primed and all gauges set, the engine should start.

I think it started on the second try.

My heart was pounding as I quickly hopped back in the plane, careful not to walk into the turning propeller.

I contacted the tower after taxiing to the active runway and we were once again off and climbing to a flight level of 4500ft. But not without further adventure. As we flew over Lloydminster, Alberta, the weather was closing in. The forecast called for partly cloudy with occasional snow squalls in the area, but nothing too bad. That would change.

Snow was now blowing in through the vents and coming into the cockpit.
I had been reducing our altitude to stay below cloud level.
We were flying VFR or Visual Flight Rules, meaning that we must see the ground at all times and remain 500 feet or more below the cloud level or ceiling.
As you travel west from the prairies, the ground actually rises above sea level all the way to the Rocky Mountains.
This means that as I am forced to fly lower to stay out of the clouds, the ground is actually coming up to meet us.
I was never good at math, but was very aware that this was not a good situation.
As we flew over the Vermillion Airport, I thought how odd and dangerous that there was a water tower pretty much in line with the active runway.
It may very well be what saved our lives.
Ten minutes past the airport and having to fly lower to maintain visual, it happened.
Complete white out. Just like flying in a milk bottle, no reference to the ground or sky.
This is how most aircraft accidents (deaths) happen.
The pilot loses visibility and reference to the ground. The confusion of having your airspeed going up and your altimeter telling you that you are going down tricks your brain into pulling back on the controls.

If you are in a turning attitude and you keep pulling back on the control column, you put the aircraft into a spiral spin. Pulling tighter and tighter as your airspeed increases and your altitude drops off all the way into a smoking hole in the ground.

"Visual Flight Rule" Pilots are trained not to look out the window and to only read their instruments.
This is easier said than done!
You are taught to do what is called a timed turn. It is the best procedure when faced with the situation of a white out.
A timed turn is a turn in which the clock and the turn coordinator are used to change heading a definite number of degrees in a given time.
For example, in a standard-rate turn (3° per second), an airplane turns 45° in 15 seconds; in a half-standard-rate turn, the airplane turns 45° in 30 seconds. It is a primitive but effective way to get yourself 180° back to where you have come from.
I was about to start counting steamboats while holding my altitude and turn and bank indicator at 45°.
I leveled the wings as my heading was reversed to 90° the opposite heading and kept my eyes on my instruments.
This is the tricky part of flying VFR and trusting your instruments.
Staying level until the ground would reappear.
Well thank the heavens it did, and I almost immediately spotted the water tower.
I knew that if I flew directly over the water tower, I should see the runway up ahead.
It was snowing harder now and I was on a final approach to the airfield, but could not see far enough ahead to know for sure that a runway would appear.

The elevation of Vermillion Airport is 1900 feet above sea level. I was at 2000 feet when I spotted what looked like a runway through the blowing snow.
I corrected my approach and successfully landed the plane. Once down on the ground, we could not see any buildings or where to turn off of the active runway.
All we could see was the edge of the runway just under the wing, so we followed it until there was a turn off.
As I taxied the Cessna blindly through the blowing snow, there emerged a large grey shape.
It was the airport terminal.
When we walked in the doors of the airport, I heard someone ask, "Where did you come from?"
My mom and I had survived a terrible situation. I laid down on a bench and closed my eyes.
What a day!
I believe that knowledge of systems and check lists are what saved us that day.

Every business owner should use proven systems and check lists to be ready for the unknown.
This book provides proven strategies and systems that will prepare your business to be sold and check lists to ensure that you are ready for a wonderful retirement.

www.riskdoctor.ca

Timing is Everything

Following TSX/Dow Jones over the past 25 years.
There was *"Boom Bust and Echo"*. Boomers where going to change the markets and devalue stocks.
There have been many perceived catastrophic events. In October 1987 people were jumping out of buildings and helicopters as the markets fell drastically over a few days. Black Monday they called it.
Leveraged investors believed that they had lost everything, and that their world was over.
The Canadian market actually fell 28% over that period, only to recover within a few months.
How about the Tech bubble of 2000?
I had met investors that believed that their portfolios were well diversified by using three different financial advisors and owning ten different technology funds.
The technology sector would actually be the only investment sector that could not recover from its lofty heights.
Then there was 9-11.
Who could imagine terrorists taking out the financial district of the United States and the events that followed? Again, Airlines stocks, Investment dealers and people continued on with life, family and investing.
Then there was the banking collapse of 2008.
If I was to imagine the worst thing possible for equity markets that could happen, it would be a global banking disaster.
Well, as time has shown, even this was not enough to kill business around the world, only a blip on the long term investing chart.
I do not mean to down play these horrible events in American history, my point being we as North Americans press onward and upward.
The S&P 500 is at new highs as of this writing.
Real estate prices have rebounded across the U.S.

The first black U.S. president has served a term and set precedent for generations to come.
Wars will happen and political events will put fear into us all, but they will have little effect on the long term investor.
When we look at the time frame 1980 - 2014 we find that markets are going to double every ten years due to the planet's need for goods and services.
Equity investments or business are the only true way to out-perform inflation.
Having said that, **diversification** is the only safe way to grow an investment portfolio and your net worth.
As business owners, we plow profits back into our business, sometimes neglecting to diversify and plan for our future.
Although this book is about selling your business and living from the proceeds of your "life time of work", you will find many references to the importance of advice.
Surrounding yourself with a team of professionals to leverage the knowledge and experience is of paramount importance.
Seeking the advice of an experienced planner is key for goal setting, tax planning and risk management.
This book is intended to be a self help overview and guide for success, but don't try to do it all yourself.
I do not do my own personal dentistry, accounting or auto maintenance.
I go to the best because I want satisfaction.
There is nothing worse than spending money on something and being disappointed.
There is nothing worse than reinventing the wheel, only to find that you are wasting valuable time trying to resolve issues.
Time truly is money.
The time you spend managing your money should be your first priority every year.
Meet with your planner for a review.
Make sure that you are not paying too much tax.
You will never get that money back.

Watch your net worth grow and your family change.
You will find that you are off course most of the time.
Making corrections and adjustments along the way will get you to the desired destination.
Start your year with a written plan.
Use proven tools to visualize your path.
The web page http://www.nobrowndays.com is a proven success formula.
Take time to visualize your goals and to know what it is that you want in retirement.
Many people spend more time planning a vacation each year than they do planning the rest of their lives.

From my family to yours, good health and prosperity.
Enjoy the book.

Chapter 1.

Selling Your Business
Darren's Story

Darren Cole is another success story that came with hard work and family influence.

As a young teen in Duncan, British Columbia, Darren's first job was sweeping the parking lot of the restaurant directly across the street from his home.

Although he was only paid in free pizza, it was something that he enjoyed and it gave him a challenge each day to keep the lot clean. His father had always instilled, "Do your best", and he remembers trying to get every last pebble of debris from that parking lot.

From parking lot sweeper to kitchen helper and eventually assisting the serving staff, he was working his way up the responsibility chain and building trust with the owners.

Darren remembers when the owners purchased the land beside the restaurant and expanded the parking lot.

He used to play soccer in that lot, and thankfully was no longer responsible for keeping it clean.

Darren ended up working in numerous restaurants, and would become a shareholder in many.

At the time of writing, Darren is the sole owner of Steeples restaurant, a converted United Church in the bedroom community in Shawnigan Lake, B.C., approximately 45 minutes from the capital city of Victoria.

Since buying out his partners in 2008, he has won many awards for both culinary expertise and service.

"It was time to move on," he explains to me in our December 2014 telephone interview.

"The economy and strict new drinking laws have done nothing to help the hospitality industry."

"I put the restaurant up for sale in the summer of 2013 and registered for a program that had been established by our Provincial Government.
http://www.welcomebc.ca/Immigrate/About-the-BC-PNP/Investing-in-B-C.aspx
P.N.P. found me a buyer from overseas. They made me an offer in October 2013 and were to take over the business in December of 2013.
I am still waiting for the paperwork to be complete and for the new owners to take over.
The program, although I am sure is a great way to bring foreign money into our country and province, and provides a way for Canadians to retire from their business, is incredibly under-staffed and the processing and transactions are taking years to implement."
So Steeples Restaurant has been in limbo for over a year now, while Darren keeps promoting and offering new dining experiences for his faithful customers.

~

Selling a small or medium sized business is a complex and emotional undertaking.
Value isn't an easy thing to figure out.
For one thing, there is not going to be much to compare to and previously sold businesses do not share information publicly for small business.
There is no MLS-like database on previous sales transactions.
This is where using a business broker can bring good value.
A good business valuation requires gathering information, lots of information.
A proper evaluator will need to establish as many comparable industry facts as will be available.

Changes in every industry are rapid, so information that is more than one year old may be irrelevant.
Is the industry booming or declining?
How easy is it for competitors to enter the market?
What is your business market share?
What is your relationship with customers, suppliers and bankers?
Are the hard assets such as land or buildings included in the sale?
If you are looking to sell all or part of your business, you will need to have a good idea of the value of the business.
In this chapter I will help you to understand the different approaches to business valuation.
You must remember that your prospective buyer or share purchaser will also be using a method of valuing your company. Somewhere in between you must strike a deal.
The process of determining the value is called valuation.
You and the buyer or investor need to determine what you feel is an appropriate business valuation because it will be the basis for negotiating.
Valuation is not an exact science, and there are different ways of valuing a business.
Each of these methods is based on different assumptions and financial information, which typically results in a different value for each method.
My preference is to focus on cash flows, both current and historical.
To find a business in a sector that is expanding and has great potential for growth.
The video rental industry for instance has long since past. Remember Block Buster?
Times change in the blink of an eye.
Do you remember your first cell phone?

I think mine was $3500 and was hard mounted into my car.
At the time of this writing, the European Space Agency has landed a spacecraft named Philae on a comet.
A ten year mission successfully accomplished on November 12, 2014. For complete story **http://www.space.com/27697-rosetta-comet-landing-full-coverage.html**
Be sure that your business is not losing ground.
Human knowledge is doubling every 12 months.
In 1943, it was documented that human knowledge was doubling every 25 years.
Now it is estimated that with technologies such as the internet, people will double their knowledge every 13 months.
And it is anticipated by the end of the century to double every 12 hours.
You need to keep up with the times.
If you are not keeping up, you are falling behind.
Any business can be bought for the right price and turned around to be a great investment.
But you need to know what you are doing.
Paying for cash flow is a preferred method of valuation.
In this chapter we will talk about all methods of establishing a business value.

Discounted cash flow method is usually the most accurate and simple way to estimate a business value.
Discounted cash flow pertains to the anticipated future cash flow based on current and past cash flows.
This method can achieve how much the business is worth today, what the buyers' anticipated rate of return will be and or how much equity or share amounts the investor will receive for their investment.

It is more accurate than some methods because of the importance of cash flow, but also the value is discounted based on the risk involved and rates of return that would be guaranteed without other investment vehicles.

The investor is going to be rewarded for his investment both in return on investment (share value) and company earnings. Ups and downs are taken into effect and built into the discounted value.

Top down example of discounted cash flow method:

What if I have $100,000 to invest for a five year period and I am looking for the best return on my investment.

The bank will offer a guaranteed rate over the same time period.

I review the books of ABC Company and reveal that my ROI or Return On Investment will be three times greater based on the discounted cash flow method of pricing ABC Co.

I am able to make an informed decision.

Investors are looking to be compensated for their risk, and their benchmark rate — or "discount rate" — will adjust for the value of money over time.

They will choose a discount rate and compare your proposal against that rate.

The discounted cash flow method allows values to be estimated even when your cash flow is fluctuating.

A start-up or new venture may expect to lose money in the first few years and then make money in later years.

This is taken into account.

This method is only as good as the information you receive from earnings.

It is bit complex and may require a professional to assist.

The risk lies in the future earnings and information you start with.

The discount or adjustment to value is dependent on this and other factors depending on the business.

As a purchaser I will want to know what my potential return on investment will be before I decide to invest in ABC Company.

To do this I must compare the amount that I will earn at the end of my five years to that of a guaranteed investment.

The only way to do this is to project estimated cash flow in the final year and the estimated value of the business at that time, calculate the value of my shares and determine my rate of return.

I must also remember that shares in this company are not liquid.

I will need to find a buyer or have an exit strategy.

Going-concern value method calculates your business value based on how cash flow increases in the future like discounted cash flow, compares the current investment to the future (cash inflows).

Revenues of previous years are used to project future revenues. It assumes those revenues will not change.

Book Value method is the net worth, or the shareholders' equity of your business as shown in its financial statements. Subtracting your liabilities from your assets gives you your net worth or book value.

Book value can be used to show past values, increases and gains.

It will also be used to show shareholders' equity.

Liquidation value method is often used to sell a business to satisfy its creditors.

With the exception of land, any assets using this method will be greatly discounted.
They may have greater value than the liquidation value method.
They can also be called distressed values. Liquidation value does not reflect the real worth of an asset.
As you can see, arriving at a fair market price or your company's true value is a daunting task.
My bottom line is that "The value of a business in only what someone is willing to pay for it." Increasing its value is key.
Your ability to attract qualified buyers and negotiate an agreed upon value or selling price vastly improves with knowledge.
I trust that in this book you will learn some lessons and that you will increase the current value and receive fair market value for your business when you sell.
It may be wise to enlist the help of someone that has done this before.
As a purchaser of this book, you are entitled to my free Financial Planning Calculator.
A Complete Retirement, Budgeting, Tax Planning and Risk Management analysis in one application.
You will also receive "Business Viewpoint", the first in a series of financial planning booklets for your financial future, part of a complete financial planning system.
What are you doing after work?

Visit www.riskdoctor.ca for your free financial calculator and Personal Viewpoint Planning Booklet

Chapter 2.

Ian's Story
Taxation of your Business

Ian grew up in the popular farming community of Crystal City, a southern Manitoba town near the United States border. Crystal City is a hard working farming community known for its curlers and baseball players.

Ian started a Hay Brokerage business back in 1993 with the help of a neighbour who was doing the same.

The neighbour mentioned to Ian that there was enough of a market for the both of them in this industry, so Ian began the hard work of establishing HayBusters.

By 1995, he had developed a reputation for providing quality Alfalfa, Grass Hay or Straw to the many feed customers across North America.

His experience with various farmers and what they used for feeding livestock would allow him to recommend quality and proper feeds to others.

At this time, the focus was on purchasing and selling quality hay not just for dairy, beef and horses, but also goat, sheep and white tailed deer.

Finding and transporting hay throughout North America and building trust with his customers is the foundation of his business. However the feed needs to be covered and Ian also is a leading provider of Tarps.

These tarps come in a variety of sizes, but certainly are larger than what you would purchase at your local hardware store. Years of hard work have allowed for Ian to semi-retire as a relatively young man.

Currently the business operations are run with one key administrative employee (who has been with him for the past 12 years) and one key person in the field building and maintaining customer relationships.

With annual sales of $2.5 million last year, Ian is looking into selling the business as a going concern.

Ian is looking to find a manager that will purchase shares over a period of years eventually buying him out completely.

His plans to sell have been in motion for a number of years, allowing the time required in which to structure the most tax efficient succession plan with his accountant.

Ian recommends using the best accounting firm that you can find, and to give yourself plenty of time prior to the date of purchase to make the required adjustments to your corporate structure.

Remember that it may take time to prepare the restructuring of share ownership and to maximize family capital gains distribution. Using the best taxation specialists available to assist with planning is essential and can save hundreds of thousands of dollars that would otherwise go to Revenue Services. Keep your money in the family!

Whether you're passing the company on to a family member or selling to outside interests, you will require a business valuation that establishes a realistic and fair price.

This value will be an important focal point of your transition plan.

Valuating a business is not a simple task.

The number you have in mind may differ from that of your family successors, potential buyers or tax assessors.

It's probably best to call in a specialist who can look at your assets, liabilities and goodwill with clear-eyed detachment.

Different methods can be used to arrive at your business valuation, and they can be used alone or in combination.

Selling or transferring equity to a family member is unique in its nature and has its own challenges and intricacies.

Maintaining the company's goals strategies and structure will have greater chance of continuity if the family member has spent a great deal of time working within the business. Understanding the culture and values created over the life of the company may be important to the family business.

These otherwise invisible characteristics of family firm's values and culture will often be lost if shares are sold to outside interests.

Studies have been done on the Family Business and how values can be retained.

If this is a concern for your family, the article "Values in Family Business" by Ritch L. Sorenson may be of value to you. Published in the SAGE Handbook of Family Business in 2014, it will provide an overview of values-related research in the organizational behavior discipline.

* **Chapter Tip:** *Allow time for sale of the business and maximize Canada's Lifetime Capital Gains Exemption is a topic of prime importance. Structure the ownership to ensure that shares qualify and in certain circumstances multiplying the exemption among family members can save the owner hundreds of thousands of dollars. Select an established and reputable Business Accountant.*

SMALL BUSINESS SUCCESSION - The "Anti" Freeze

By Chris Geldert, CA.

There is an ancient Chinese proverb which roughly translates to "Wealth does not pass three generations" and has an equivalent in many cultures.

History is littered with examples of this and none more spectacular than the rise and fall of the Roman Empire. Granted the rise and fall of the Roman Empire took significantly longer than three generations, there were definitely three distinct parts: the creation of the Roman Republic, transformation of the Republic into the Roman Empire, and lastly the fall of the Roman Empire.

With such incredible historic examples, it should then come as no surprise the life of the family business follows a similar pattern.

Statistics tell us only 30% of family businesses survive the transition to the second generation and only a mere 10% to the third.

In planning for their exit strategy the business owner is left with two options to consider:

1. Sale of the business. This can be to a competitor, existing management, or in rare circumstances to a child or other family member; or
2. Transfer of the business to a successor without a sale. The successor could be the children, existing management, or a combination of both.

Is it possible that the fall of the family business is being aided by sound tax planning solutions?

The following article explores how estate freezes may actually work against the best interests of the business and the family.

Overview of the Estate Freeze

The estate freeze is a popular strategy as it provides for an extremely tax-efficient transfer of the business to the successors(s), typically the child(ren) of the owner. This planning tool allows the successor, that is the child(ren), to participate in the future growth of the business without having to risk their own capital, while simultaneously locking in the value to the owner (parent). The locked-in value provides a level of certainty of the future tax liability in respect to the business owner's shares which can only decrease over time. The strategy itself does not provide immediate liquidity and needs to be supplemented with additional strategies to monetize the value in the future.
In a typical estate freeze the business owner would exchange their common (growth) shares of the corporation on a tax-free basis for preferred shares ("freeze shares") which would have a specified value equal to the fair market value ("FMV") of the common shares at the time of the freeze. The successor, either directly or through a trust, would then subscribe for new common shares of the corporation for a nominal amount.

Pitfall of the Estate Freeze

The ability to transfer the ownership of the business tax-free can be so appealing it perpetuates the idea the legacy of the family is the business.
This focus can lead to strategic decisions which trump the goal of creating value. Even the well-intentioned estate freeze can end up being the catalyst to the fall of the family business and family discord. Before implementing an estate freeze please consider the following:

1. The parents often implement the freeze at a time when they are looking to slow down and enjoy the fruits of their labour. For many owners, the equity accumulated within the business will become a key component in retirement. Since the estate freeze does not provide liquidity a separate strategy becomes necessary for funding the retirement. One such strategy is to have the preferred shares received by virtue of the freeze, redeemed over a period of time. While effective, this strategy has the unintended result of placing undue stress on the child(ren) and complicating the company's finances.

2. Part of the estate freeze entails the child(ren) receiving shares for no consideration. Not having to go through the same trials and tribulations as the parents nor having to risk any of their own assets may lead to questionable commitment.

3. Parents often view their children through rose coloured glasses and find it hard to be objective when it comes to their true abilities. Genetics does not ensure aptitude which means the child(ren) may not be the best choice to lead the business. Consider this: when companies look outside for a CEO the list can start with thousands of candidates before it is whittled down to 5-10 who receive in-depth interviews. Statistically the odds are against the child(ren) being the best choice to continue maximizing the value of the business.

4. Family members not involved in the business often end up resenting those who continue in the business, regardless if they are successful.

Create a Business Solution

With all the potential issues a wiser strategy might be to monetize the value of the business through a sale. This is not to say that the sale cannot be made to the child(ren) as long as it occurs at fair market value. By agreeing to purchase the business the child(ren) are showing their commitment and belief in the future of the business. Selling to a third-party might perturb the child(ren) at first. This frustration is quickly eased when the children learn that mom and dad will be receiving millions of dollars, some of which might be allocated to them immediately or used to ensure a significant inheritance.

Still Considering an Estate Freeze

A properly structured estate freeze provides many benefits and has worked well for numerous families. The key is to understand and consider the potential risks involved. The key trait among families who successfully implement this type of planning is plenty of open and frank dialogue among family members.
They strive to understand the family dynamics and focus on passing along family values.
Among the conversation includes clearly outlining what is expected from the child(ren) who want to work in and possibly own the business. Several have gone so far as to establish panels from their trusted advisors to provide an unbiased opinion of the child's abilities, commitment and desire. The parents also gave significant thought as to how they would compensate the children both involved in the business and those excluded from involvement.

So before implementing an estate freeze consider what your legacy will be.

This article was provided courtesy of Chris Geldert, CA.
Chris is one of many professionals working with Family Integrity Corporation.
If you have a question for Chris, please contact myself through our Victoria offices.
www.riskdoctor.ca

Chapter 3.

How to Improve the Value of your Company

Ten steps to improve the value of your company:

Selling a business sucks.
It is a challenging process that can take years.
Emotional challenges of handing over your life's work, bringing in someone to take over the business and do it differently can take its toll. If you are selling the business to retire or a decline in health is forcing you to step down, making cosmetic changes to a company at the last minute before putting it on the market is a recipe for disappointment. One way of enhancing value is to increase sales (the "top line") and to reduce expenses such as owner perks to improve the "bottom line."
Whether you've done the valuation yourself or had it done by a professional, once you've arrived at a realistic number, it's only reasonable to wonder how that number can be improved. Keep in mind that your business may be worth more in pieces than as a whole.
There are many ways to enhance the value of your company prior to your business succession .
It may be in your best interest to find a qualified business valuator prior to implementing changes. Change will take time and analysing where to start and where to get best value in the time frame you seek will be beneficial.
A review of your business plan and designing a Strategic Plan is highly recommended. (See Chapter 6.)

A professional valuation will contribute to a smooth transition and continued harmony among purchaser and your employees and family members.

* Remember that valuation is not a science and that a business is only worth what someone is willing to pay for it.

Step one:
Seek advice
An experienced third party can sometimes see the business from a different light, and bring new and positive ideas for you to increase the sale-ability and value .

Step Two:
Profits are crucial
If the business is just breaking even, don't expect a high offer.
Don't suck the life out of your business.
If you have retained earnings in the business, this is a good thing and it will show that your business is profitable.
Be mindful that you are not fed up and giving up on your business.
You will know when you have had enough of the business. This is a sign to make change and the real work of turning it around should begin.
Remember that if it has little or no value, it is up to you to change this.
I like the terms "Look Top Down" rather than "Bottom Up". Work "on your business" rather than "in your business".
Build the business to be attractive and with potential for growth. Make a plan. Never give up!

Step Three:
Increase sales and lower expenses
This seems like a no-brainer but is most important when preparing for sale. Look for ways to increase efficiency.

Step Four:
A well designed business plan can be shared with your potential purchaser. But be careful not to divulge too much information, rather use it as a teaser.
Do you have a Strategic Plan?

Step Five:
Continue to invest and improve
Be careful not to burn out when things get busy.
If you have a five year plan to sell and things are going well, it is the perfect time to bring in a manager or to promote from within. Delegate all duties possible. Become your own personal promoter and do the things that you do best. Try to focus on what you are good at and what you did in the beginning. Start to look **top down** at your business and get away from working **in your business**.

Step Six:
Develop a strategic plan
S.W.O.T. is a structured planning method used to evaluate the **strengths, weaknesses, opportunities and threats.** See the strategic planning chapter of this book and give your business credibility as a growing concern with long-term potential.

Step Seven:
Develop systems and processes for each area of your business.

You may need to re-evaluate each of these processes and teach new efficiencies to your staff.
You want to create a business that can survive without you. To do this, you may have to provide training and motivation to your people.
Have an open door policy, to hear what your staff have to say.
Work to solve any internal conflicts immediately.
Benefit plans will help to attract and maintain quality employees.
Keep employee turnover to a minimum.
Pay close attention to your management team.
Do not micromanage if at all possible.
Build a strong and professional team, this will add great value to your business.

Step Eight:
Understand Social Media
If you do not have a web presence, you are dead in the water. When was the last time you opened the yellow pages to find a product or service? GOOGLE is your friend.
Get testimonials from your long term clients of friends.
Stand out from the crowd.
Get involved with local social clubs and make them aware of the improvements of your business.
In many ways, selling your company is also a marketing challenge. That's why it's important to showcase to potential buyers whatever differentiates your product or service from the competition.
Create a company mission statement and make it visible to everyone that enters your establishment.

Ask some of your long-time clients for testimonials explaining why they are doing business with you and what keeps them coming back.

Regardless to whether you actually go through with a sale, these tips will help you build a stronger, more efficient and valuable company.

Step Nine:
Making sure that you have a plan for work and that you work your plan is important, but why are you doing this?

For your family of course. You need to understand that you are the provider for your family and when you have accumulated enough assets, you will not have to work again. That may or may not be your goal, but you should understand what it is that you are wanting from your life.

Your legacy depends on it.

What do you want to be remembered for?

What is the most important thing to you?

You may say family. You may say church. You may say your golf game. Either way, you need to understand why you are focusing on your future and what it will bring.

It is only when you know where you are headed and why you are heading that way, that you can truly enjoy your success.

Step Ten:
Recognize that you are building your business to be run without you. Realize that your employees are your most important asset, or soon will be. Focus on family and health. Each of those people that you are responsible for are family members. Do you have a health plan for their families

Chapter 4

Clem's Story and the Importance of Employees

Clem and I met a very long time ago.
I was a rookie financial advisor looking to build my business and Clem was getting married to his lovely wife, Wendy.
They had just purchased their first home in St. Vital, a suburb of Winnipeg, Manitoba.
Clem and Wendy had attended a Welcome Wagon Bridal Show in Winnipeg way back in the Spring of 1989. They had entered their names into a draw at the booth I had set up at the Bridal Show. About one month later I called them to set up an appointment to introduce myself. One week later I showed up at their door to explain how I had nothing to sell them, and could be of value to them at some point in the future.
Clem had been working with Future Ventilation for a couple of years at that time, having started with this company shortly after high school.
We talked about savings and life insurance.
About how time was on their side and the magic of compounding interest.
We could start planning for the future and should purchase some life insurance now while they were young and had their health.
We started with $25 per month into a Universal Life contract with Metropolitan Life.
Clem followed Future Ventilation when the company moved to Kelowna B.C. in 2002.

At this time the name changed to Excel Ventilation, as there was already a company that was using the name "Future". The original owners realized that the best succession and retirement plan would be to offer key employees a share package at certain times.

These shares would be a percentage of the value of the company at that given time.

Clem bought shares over a thirteen year period and is currently the major share holder.

He has already eyed up potential partners for his exit strategy. Offering shares in small parcels over the length of a career was definitely a wise move by both owner and employee.

Excel Ventilation has grown to be a major player in Western Canada, building hospitals, airports and schools.

All partners of Excel Ventilation are protected through the use of a buy-sell agreement.

This insurance policy protects all owners in the event of death of one of the partners.

A lump sum of money comes from the insurance company to purchase the shares from the surviving spouse.

I have been able to establish a very competitive employee benefit package for Clem and Excel Ventilation.

Clem agrees that it is very important to those employees that are raising a family.

The dental, disability and life insurance coverage forms a part of the Excel Ventilation Company Policy with regards to those that work for Excel.

For added flexibility and to curb costs, we implemented a Private Health Spending Account for each partner and employee, a little know non-taxable benefit that an employee can use for most health or vision claims.

Clem says, "An employee benefit plan is great for keeping employees and looking after their families, I think every company should offer a plan.

The benefit of a Private Health Spending Account has been great for controlling costs.

As our staff grow older the traditional health plan costs can go up by as much as 30% and this was shared with the employee. Although not the best solution for everyone, it proves to be the most efficient method for the majority."

As his financial advisor, I have watched Clem build a wonderful family and successful business.

We have worked together accumulating assets both personally and with his corporation.

It has truly been a pleasure working with such good people.

Employee Morale
Ideally you want the right people to stay on board and help make your company grow.

Develop a human relations plan that focuses on your company Mission Statement.

Share your success and concerns with your employees at year end.

Training:
Training in group settings with your existing employees will create camaraderie and a level playing field from which to grow.

Sharing knowledge of skill sets and training for technological changes will upgrade staff skills and keep your company competitive.

Put training strategies into your Strategic Plan, and make it a regular event.

Make H.R. a part of the S.W.O.T. that will be talked about in chapter six.

You can develop training strategies that are in line with your company's skill requirements and ensure these are linked to your performance evaluation.

If you find it difficult to make time for a corporate training session, find a web based program that employees are able to do individually.

Keep in mind that training or interactive workshops can pay dividends and should not be a passing thought.

Let employees know of your business plan and how this will be incorporated into the long term planning process.

Show them your strategies and develop a rewards a program for maintaining loyalty to your company.

Perks, rewards and benefits are sure ways to keep good people and will improve morale.

Provide profit sharing or smaller family rewards such as entertainment vouchers or appreciation dinners.

Promote exercise and a healthy work place which can increase productivity by 4 - 15%.

Simply using a hand sanitizer at work can reduce your sick days by 21%.

Look into a Private Health Spending Account. They are totally flexible and what you pay into your employee account will provide a tax free benefit to you and your employees.

Watch this three minute video to explain how it works:
http://www.winflex.ca/david-shortill

Chapter 5.

<u>Your Company Policy</u>
<u>Insuring your Greatest Assets</u>

This chapter will be all about your feelings toward those that are working for and with you and your company.
Your responsibility to them and their families.
It is one thing to focus on recruiting and the retaining of key employees, it is another to realize that they are your greatest asset.
I want you to imagine taking a one month vacation from the company. It will be difficult not to worry about the daily ups and downs that you know are going to happen while you are away.
Each day you are lying on the beach trying not to call your manager to see how things are going is difficult.
After one month you return only to find that everything is fine, as it was when you left and there is even some good news on how things were handled when it got busy.
This is the company that you have built or are striving for.
A true "going concern".
Assuming that you are going to have your business run like a true investment should run.
What are you doing to protect this asset?
A company policy is in order.
A Company Policy with regards to each employee that is a part of your team.
A part of your asset, and your business.

This policy will be a written statement that is testament to your respect and will to provide for those that make their living working in your business.
What is your company policy if one of your employees is to get sick, disabled or dies?

What is your company policy if your manager has children and they need glasses or medicine?
These risks can be addressed using a Company Benefit plan. You will find that an affordable, tax deductable plan will help to maintain and attract quality employees.
It will be the answer to the responsibility that you share with the families that are helping to build your company.
I have had clients that did not take action on a company policy and one day a certain employee did not show up for work.
His name and tragic story on the radio and in the newspapers the next day.
The family left to struggle financially while dealing with the pain of loss. A company policy with regards to anyone that works for you can address these issues.

- Disability
- Life insurance (Employee and spouse)
- Critical Illness
- Dental and Health care including vision
- Retirement planning and profit sharing

The following pages are going to explain the many areas you may wish to discuss with your advisor.
They will answer the questions about
"Your Company Policy" with regards to employees and the future of your company.
There is no time like the present to review or build your Company Policy.
You will be surprised at how important this is to increasing your company's value and improving morale.

www.riskdoctor.ca

Your Company Policy with regards to:

Key person insurance

Your company policy can also address the risks of losing a key employee and how that will affect your business.

A company's most valuable assets are its people.

The loss of an owner or key employee is likely to disrupt the firm's operations and create financial loss.

To protect the firm against such loss, Key Person Insurance is purchased on the life of such owners or key employees.

It will provide tax free dollars to replace lost business income, assure creditors and employees that the business will remain a going concern and cover special expenses such as finding, securing and training a suitable replacement.

It will pay death benefits to the employee's family if desired.

Overhead insurance

A policy can be put in place to cover the overhead of your business should you or an employee become disabled for an extended period of time.

This type of policy is inexpensive and is tax deductable.

* Talk to your advisor.

Buy/Sell Agreement

An insured Buy/Sell Agreement allows for a smooth transfer of ownership when an owner dies.

The business (or surviving owners) receives cash equal to the value of the deceased's business interest in order to buy that interest. It creates a market for each owner's business interest at fair price. It assures creditors and employees of the continuation of the business in the event of an owner's death or disability. The working capital of the business will remain untouched.

Business loan insurance
Adequate debt-financing is often difficult to achieve for a small business.
Creditors may require that a loan be personally guaranteed. Business Loan Insurance assures creditors of the debt repayment without making the deceased's estate or heirs liable for the outstanding balance.
It improves the business ability to negotiate loans.
It ensures that the estate does not become liable for the loan.
It guarantees insurance dollars to pay off the loan obligation.
If the plan is properly set up, the premiums are tax deductible by the company.

Group Insurance
Group insurance is a plan between the insurer and the employer in which a number of employees can be insured under master contract.
It aids in attracting and retaining quality employees.
It reduces cost and administration.
Contributions are tax deductible to the employer and, generally, non-taxable to the employee.
It shifts obligation from the employer to the insurer in the event of catastrophic event.

Salary Continuation
A salary continuation plan is a guarantee that the employees will receive a percentage of their salary should they become disabled.
It aids in attracting and retaining key employees.
The disabled employee's salary is paid with insurance dollars.
Premiums paid are tax deductible when paid to a special health plan set up for this purpose.
Benefits can also be made available to the company in order to hire and train replacement personnel.

Deferred Compensation
A Deferred Compensation Plan is a contractual arrangement between the employer and selected employees to pay benefits in the future (at retirement, death or disability).
It provides additional benefits over and above those permissible through registered plans.
It aids in attracting and retaining key employees.
No prior approval is required from Revenue Canada.
It is an attractive form of compensation for highly taxed executives/employees.
The policy proceeds are received tax-free by the business if the employee dies.

Split-Dollar Plan
A Split-Dollar Plan is an arrangement between two parties in which the business assists the employee in paying premiums for a life insurance policy.
The business is reimbursed from the resulting proceeds whenever the policy terminates.
A unique benefit that will aid in the retention and attracting key employees.
The amount advanced the policy is secured by the policy's cash value.
It is a low cost insurance for key employees and provides a source of loans at a very low cost. Usually 2%.

Retirement Planning
A Registered Retirement Savings Plan is simply a personal pension program.
It allows you to save, tax deferred, a portion of your annual income in order to build up a substantial "nest egg" for retirement.
An RRSP builds up equity during the life of the plan to ensure maintenance of a comfortable standard of living in your retirement years.

Neither the contributions to, nor the earnings of the plan are taxable until the plan is collapsed.

Funding the RRSP through an annuity reduces cost and administration. It also guarantees the rate and amount received at retirement.

Contributions in your spouse's name may also be tax deductible. (Spousal RRSP)

Important to talk to your Advisor about this.

Deferred Profit Sharing Plan

A Deferred Profit Sharing Plan permits employers to reward selected key employees.

The employer's payments can be calculated by reference to business profits.

A trustee receives the employer's tax deductible payments on the employee's behalf and all income earned by the trust is tax deferred.

Employees are rewarded without being pushed into higher tax brackets.

Funding a DPSP with an annuity provides increased settlement flexibility and a guaranteed lifetime income.

Payments by the business are immediately tax deductible. Funds are automatically allocated for each member of the plan.

Chapter 6.

Strategic Planning and S.W.O.T
Azam's story

I got to know Azam and his story one fall evening sitting in the front seat of his truck.
Having eaten his incredible food for years, I thought that perhaps he would have a story to tell.
Well, you are about to find out.
A mutual friend introduced us a few days prior to our meeting. I called and asked if he had a few moments for an interview and that I was putting a book together, and would love to hear his story.
Azam Khan starts with the history of his family.
"Our family come from a small village called Charoona in a District called Alaga in the Northwestern Frontier Province in the Country of Pakistan. They are Afghani with roots of the Pathan. Our family are direct descendants of King Sulamon and we were the last tribe of Israel.
The people of this region have been through generations of atrocities. Often seized by the Taliban, the men are killed, women are raped and the children taken away. They call this all in the name of god, but whatever."
"We were simple people, we grow our own food, raise our own livestock in a village that is almost 600 years old. It is at an altitude of just under 3000' above sea level and about 400 miles south west of the Himalayan foot hills.
People have heard of Kashmir or the Khyber Pass. That is basically where we come from. Our family are direct descendants of Alexander the Great's soldiers. The soldiers that were left behind to raise families after his ascent through the area.
The village just got electricity about 20 years ago.
Houses are made of Buffalo shit, hay and timber."

"My Grandfather was the first to come to Vancouver Island with the Mercantile Navy on November 7, 1939.
Prior to the ship leaving to head back to Bombay India, his boss offered him a suit and $5, and told him to take it and run. So that is what he did.
After a number of years living on the lam, Sir Robert Holland of the Royal Family of England took him under his wing giving him work and a place to live in the servant quarters, eventually helping him to get his citizenship.
Once settled and working in the Saw Mills, he sent for my father. My father however, would have to elude detection in his escape from the area, and realized the only way out of town would be to climb into the cart that collected dead bodies on a regular basis and took them out of town.
So this is what he did.
He knew that the horse and carriage was going to where he needed to go and so he snuck into the carriage with the dead bodies.
Once settled, my father would eventually assist in bringing many of my cousins, relatives and friends over.
Because of him, there are now over 300 of us on the Island. Many of us settled in the Lake Cowichan area. This story was well known at the time.
Bringing our people out of the ravaged village was a team effort. My father's acquaintances were the Air Field Marshall of Pakistan, The Surgeon General Army of Pakistan, Prince Ayub of Pakistan and Miangul Aurazab, the Walleut (Prince) of SWAT."
The story is long and interesting. He eventually arrived here on the island to be with my Grandfather February 14, 1954. He was seventeen years old."

Although Azam went to school to get into the hospitality industry and worked for some esteemed corporations such as The Wedgewood, The Four Seasons, and Metropolitan Hotel in Vancouver, and later the Aerie Resort on Vancouver Island, the corporate ladder with big corporations was not for him and going into business for himself would prove to be much more rewarding.

With his first restaurant, he began catering to local stores with different products that would be sold from their delis.

He grew this business to include 52 stores offering eight different products.

Eventually catering would prove to be his passion and he closed the restaurant, took a brief hiatus and started Vancouver Island Event Catering, an elaborate food truck (trailer) that he sets up at various locations and events to cater his incredible lines of Western and Eastern cuisine.

He offers any type of food, however his family creations are outstanding.

"In the beginning it was brutal. There were days that I would make fifteen or twenty five dollars per day. Not even covering the cost of diesel for his truck.

I don't deny thinking that I wanted to quit many times, but the way people embrace and love the food, and the challenge of catering to large groups, that fuels my passion."

Since then things have grown in leaps and bounds.

He is doing more catering than lunch or dinner from the food truck and the catering contracts have tripled.

"I can see the growth, and the type of business that we are doing. Rock concerts, movie sets, clients from the interior of British Columbia, Alberta, Colorado, France and recent government contracts.

I have a vision of being the best and largest catering company on Vancouver Island."

Together we have talked about a Business Plan and a Strategic Plan for the New year.

"It is time to get a company health plan, dental and to look after my staff and family. We are currently a sole proprietor, with full intentions of incorporation in the future. The goal in the next two year will be to have a commercial kitchen on my own property. To get one more truck out into the larger market of Victoria".

Strategic Planning:

A Strategic plan is a business plan with focus on reality.
Your strategic plan will focus on S.W.O.T.
Strengths - Weakness - Opportunity - Threats
A **S.W.O.T.** analysis can be carried out for a product, place, industry or person.
It involves specifying the objective of the business venture or project and identifying the internal and external factors that are favorable and unfavorable to achieve that objective.
The primary difference between a business plan and strategic plan is that the business plan is often a static snapshot of the future.
A strategic plan, on the other hand, is more dynamic and flexible.
Strategic planning can be the designing of directions and initiatives, while a business plan can involve more tactical material, usually to achieve a specific goal.
Business planning involves details of **"how I will do it"** and includes detailed managerial aspects such as marketing, human resources, organizational structure and financial projections.
We are going to learn about strategic planning and how it pertains to selling your business.
Before building a strategic plan for your future, be sure to review risks that may set you back of your plan.
Be sure to understand what the greatest asset is to you and your family.

I would recommend that it is your ability to earn money and to be able to go to work every day and to follow through on your strategic plan.
Your health is paramount to your success.
Ask anyone that has lost their health, how important money becomes.
Your quality of life is of upmost importance.
Protecting your family assets requires some risk management.
Disability Insurance, Overhead Insurance and Critical Illness Insurance can be critical in attaining your goals.
One in three people aged 30-40 will encounter a disability that will take them out of work for more than six months.
If you are not able to work, what happens to your business?
There are many disability plans that can cover this risk and have money come in to keep the momentum of your plan in place.
Talk to your advisor about disability insurance.

Modeling
Success leaves clues!
The best way to create wealth is to "*do what wealthy people do.*"
Having worked with wealthy people and those that aspire to become financially secure, I have noticed that there is little difference in desires and/or aspirations between them and not so successful business owners.
The main difference is knowledge.
Wealthy people have worked hard at their craft, and appreciate what they have achieved just as those of us that are proud of what we have but are not successful.
Human nature is to want more. To want leisure time and family time. To want security.
When you develop your *Strategic Plan*, keep in mind that you are not doing something that has not already been done.
There have been many others that have attained the success and freedom you so desire.
Modeling yourself after others can be a great planning tool.

Look at what your competitors are doing and model your business after them.
Don't try to invent a new way to do things.
Learn from others.
Sharing ideas from successful people with those that I work with. I call it modeling.
Model yourself after those that have come before you.

S.W.O.T.
Strengths
Weakness
Opportunities
Threats
Try to list all of the business traits you can think of for each of these categories.
Then you will write down solutions and calls to action for each.
Download free S.W.O.T. template from:
http://office.microsoft.com/en-ca/templates/swot-analysis-examples-TC101875476.aspx.
Spend some time on this.
It does not have to be done in one sitting, but make it a year end process that you will share with your employees.
Better yet, have them participate in its completion over lunch.
It is gold when properly executed.

Business planning
Your business plan is not only the first thing you should have prepared prior to going into business, it is the first page of your **"how to"** get success from your business.
It is the focus on how you will do it.
Why you are doing what you do and how you will separate yourself from the rest.
Business Development Bank of Canada or BDC has plenty of written help if you are developing a new plan.
www.BDC.ca

Complete business planning is available through Family Integrity Corporation Business Viewpoint systems and management.

For the first in a series of free Business Planning Books, visit www.riskdoctor.ca or email the writer direct dave@riskdoctor.ca

Chapter 7.

Bonus: Bill Gates and Warren Buffet tips

Bill Gates on kids

1: Life is not fair – get used to it!
2: The world will expect you to accomplish something BEFORE you feel good about yourself.
3: You will NOT make $90,000 a year right out of high school.
4: If you think your teacher is tough, wait till you get a boss.
5: Flipping burgers is not beneath your dignity. Your grandparents had a different word for burger flipping: opportunity.
6: If you mess up, it's not your parents' fault, so don't whine about your mistakes – learn from them.
7: Before you were born, your parents weren't as boring as they are now. They got that way from paying your bills and listening to you talk about how cool you are.
8: Your school may have done away with winners and losers, but life HAS NOT.
9: Life is not divided into terms. You don't get summers off, and very few employers are interested in helping you "find yourself". Do that in your own time.
10: TV is not real life. In real life, people have to leave the coffee shop and go to jobs..
11: Be nice to nerds. Chances are you'll end up working for one!

Warren Buffet Advice

Have the right Heroes, the people you look up to will help form who you are to become later in life.
Invest in as much of yourself as you can, you are your own biggest asset by far.
Have your own Passion, follow it, don' t take a job if you don't like it.

Short Bio of Bill Gates: Bill Gates is the founder of Microsoft corporation; the largest software company in the world and at the time of writing this article, he is the richest man in the world. Bill Gates has held the coveted position of the world's richest man more than 12 consecutive years and he's not letting go of that position. His wealth has crossed the $100 billion mark; peaking at an all time high of $101 billion.
Bill Gates is number one on our list of the richest school drop-out billionaires; having dropped out of Harvard to start Microsoft. Though he has faced massive media attack and several anti-trust lawsuits, Bill Gates is best known for his quiet, unpretentious nature and huge donations to charity. Below are Bill Gates business quotes and advice to young entrepreneurs.

Bill Gates: 21 Quotes + Strategic Business Advice for Entrepreneurs

1. "We were young, but we had good advice good ideas and lots of enthusiasm."
2. "Our success has really been based on partnerships from the very beginning."
3. " This is a fantastic time to be entering the business world because business is going to change more in the next ten years than it has in the last fifty years."
4. "The most meaningful way to differentiate your company from your competitors, the best way to put distance between you and the crowd is to do an outstanding job with information. How you gather, manage and use information will determine whether you win or lose."
5. "A bad strategy will fail no matter how good your information is and lame execution will stymie a good strategy. If you do enough things poorly, you will go out of business."

6. "Information flow is the life blood of your company because it enables you to get the most out of your people and learn from your customers."
7. "Information work is thinking work."
8. "Business people need to shake off the notion that information is hard to get."
9. "Better information can expand the role of sales managers from being closers of big deals to being business managers."
10. "Bringing together the right information with the right people will dramatically improve a company's ability to develop and act on strategic business opportunities."
11. "A self service approach can handle 90 percent of employee administrative needs."
12. "Customer service will become the primary value added function of every business."
13. "The pace of change and the need for more personalized attention to customers will drive companies to adopt digital processes internally."
14. "As the internet drives down the cost of transactions, the middle man will disappear or evolve to add new value."
15. "Only a few businesses will succeed by having the lowest price, so most will need a strategy that includes customer services."
16. "An important re-engineering principle is that companies should focus on their core competence and outsource everything else."
17. "The competition to hire the best will increase in the years ahead. Companies that give extra flexibility to their employees will have the edge in this area."
18. "Customers want high quality at low prices and they want it now."
19. "The most important 'speed' issue is often not technical but cultural. It's convincing everyone that the company's survival depends on everyone moving as fast as possible."

20. "How fast a company can respond in an emergency is a measure of its corporate reflexes."

21. "A company's ability to respond to an unplanned event, good or bad is a prime indicator of its ability to compete."

Chapter 8.

Traits of Generation Y (The Millennials)

Wikipedia explains: Millennials (also known as the Millennial Generation or Generation Y) are the demographic cohort following Generation X.
There is no precise dates when the generation starts and ends. Researchers and commentators use birth years ranging from the early 1980's to the early 2000's.
It is from this age range that we are going to find our managers and key employees of the future.
The twenty to thirty something year old employees that will be the future of business.
This group as a whole are thinking differently.
They have different priorities.
They aren't prioritizing medical care, compared to other generations.
Yet they're the most likely to want employers who play an active role in supporting their overall health and well-being.
In fact, only 54% of this group has had a physical exam in the past 12 months compared to 60% of Generation X and 73% of Boomers.
Additional findings from a report by Aon Hewitt:

- 39% believe preventative health care is important, compared to 49% of Gen X and 69% of Boomers
- 21% participate in eating/weight management programs, compared to 23% of Gen X and 28% of Boomers; and surprisingly, 63% engage in regular exercise, compared to 52% of Gen X and 49% of Boomers.
- As banking customers, they are more than twice as likely to consider switching to a branchless bank.

- Not surprisingly, these young consumers would be open to banking with tech players like Google, Amazon and Apple if such services where offered.
- In Canada this group would bank with major telecommunications companies like Rogers, Bell or Telus.
- 55% would like help from their bank with the complicated purchase of homes or cars.
- A whopping 68% would like real time analysis of their spending and like helpful information on how and when to spend money.

Clearly this group are advanced with regards to trusting large Technological companies and they see the value of advice. They will have a grasp of technology and how it can most help your business.

Chapter 9.

The Business Viewpoint

An overview of the issues you encounter as a business owner, manager, employer, and individual, from your point of view!

For purchasing this book, you are eligible for my free financial calculator and Business Viewpoint Booklet.
Simply email me your receipt from Amazon.com or Amazon.ca, and I will forward these incredibly valuable tools.

Email: dave@riskdoctor.ca

www.riskdoctor.ca

Acknowledgments

BDC (Business Development Bank)
Ian Beavis
Warren Buffet
David Chang
Darren Cole
Wayne Cotton (Cotton Systems)
Clem Fraser
Bill Gates
Chris Geldert CA.
Azam Khan
Mom & Dad (Ralph & June Shortill)
P.N.P. (Government of British Columbia)
Standard Life
Brian Tracy (The Phoenix Seminar)
Jason Walker

www.riskdoctor.ca

www.ingramcontent.com/pod-product-compliance
Lightning Source LLC
Chambersburg PA
CBHW051821170526
45167CB00005B/2104